Minecraft Redstone

An UNOFFICIAL Kids' Guide

Percy Leed

Lerner Publications ◆ Minneapolis

Lerner Publications Company
An imprint of Lerner Publishing Group, Inc.
241 First Avenue North
Minneapolis, MN 55401 USA

For reading levels and more information, look up this title at www.lernerbooks.com.

Main body text set in Billy Infant Regular. Typeface provided by SparkType.

Library of Congress Cataloging-in-Publication Data

Names: Leed, Percy, 1968– author.
Title: Minecraft redstone : an unofficial kids' guide / Percy Leed.
Description: Minneapolis : Lerner Publications, [2023] | Series: Lightning bolt books. Minecraft 101 | Includes bibliographical references and index. | Audience: Ages 6-9 | Audience: Grades 2-3 | Summary: "Redstone is a special material in Minecraft that can be used for many things, including powering railroad tracks! From getting redstone to building circuits, readers will discover the endless opportunities of using Minecraft redstone"— Provided by publisher.
Identifiers: LCCN 2022006213 (print) | LCCN 2022006214 (ebook) | ISBN 9781728476759 (library binding) | ISBN 9781728478791 (paperback) | ISBN 9781728483467 (ebook)
Subjects: LCSH: Minecraft (Game)—Juvenile literature. | Building materials—Juvenile literature.
Classification: LCC GV1469.35.M535 L448 2023 (print) | LCC GV1469.35.M535 (ebook) | DDC 794.8/5—dc23

LC record available at https://lccn.loc.gov/2022006213
LC ebook record available at https://lccn.loc.gov/2022006214

Manufactured in the United States of America
1-52256-50696-4/15/2022

Table of Contents

Minecraft Redstone

Minecraft is a virtual game where players can choose the way they play. Players build, mine, and explore.

Redstone is a special material in *Minecraft*. It can be used to make objects, power homes, and more!

A redstone block

Finding Redstone

Players use redstone for many things, such as crafting a compass. A compass can help them make maps.

When a player wants to make an item such as a clock, they place the materials in the crafting grid of the inventory screen.

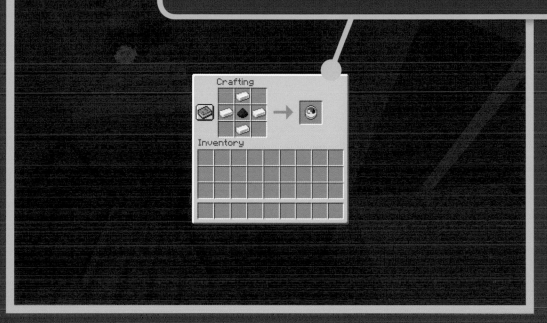

They can also use redstone to form clocks or make potions last longer. But first, a player has to find redstone. There are many ways to do this.

Players can get redstone by mining with a pickaxe. Sometimes redstone is kept in hidden chests. Another way to get redstone is by trading with a villager.

A player mines for redstone.

Redstone can be used to make armor.

Many players test their redstone creations in Creative Mode. They can try new things without being attacked by mobs.

Building Circuits

Players build circuits with redstone. Redstone circuits can make machines that do many things, including open doors.

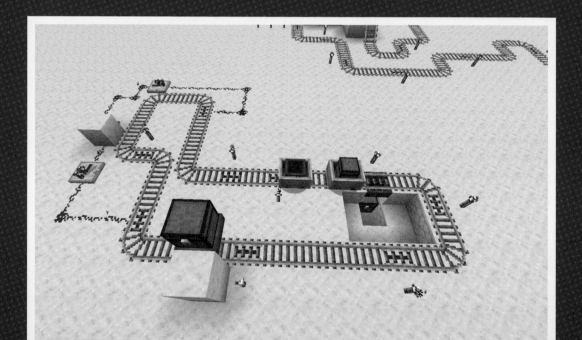

Using redstone, players can create hidden doors.

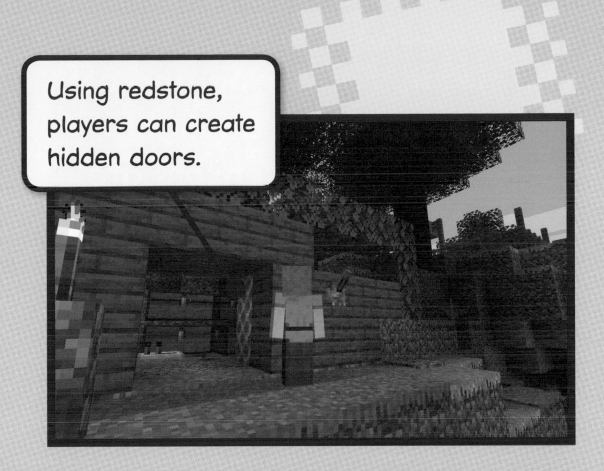

Power allows redstone circuits to light up and more. There are many ways to power redstone circuits.

Players can flip a lever to turn the circuit's power on and off. They can also use daylight sensors. Daylight sensors are powered by the sun.

The sun powers redstone lamps.

Redstone lamps in *Minecraft*

At night, players can switch the daylight sensors to night sensors. The redstone circuit will glow in the dark.

Players also use redstone circuits to set traps. Traps help catch mobs.

Building a tripwire trap is one way to catch mobs.

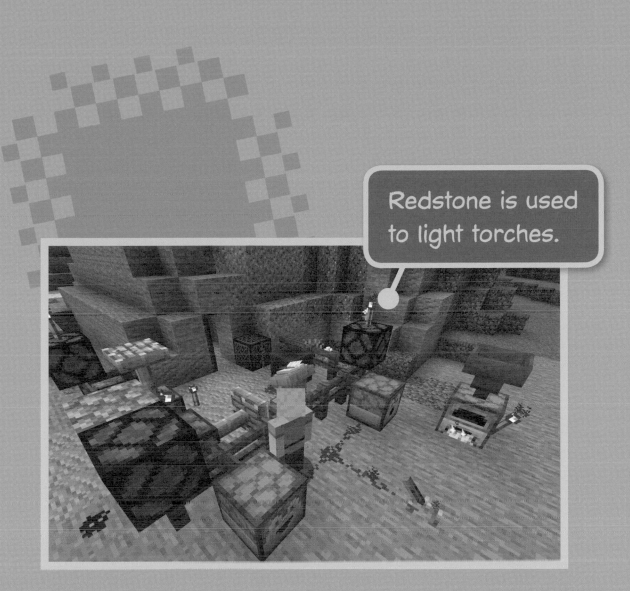

Redstone is used to light torches.

Redstone can move pistons. These devices push blocks up or out. They can move up to twelve blocks in a row.

Players can also power railroad tracks with redstone. They can place minecarts on powered rails to transport ore, build roller coasters, or go for a ride.

A player rides in a cart on railroad tracks.

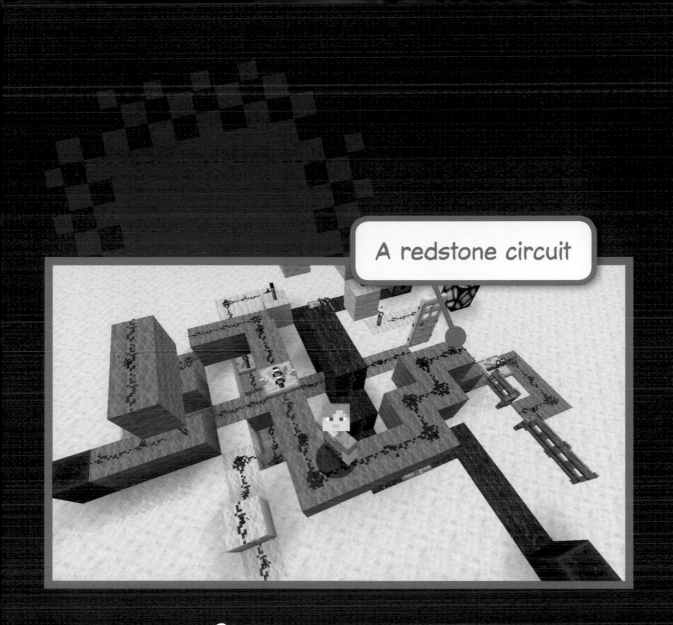

A redstone circuit

Minecraft players can try coming up with their own circuits and test their own ideas using redstone.

Fun Creations

Players have used redstone to create many fun things in *Minecraft*. They have made a working smartphone and a robot that can walk.

Some players use redstone to make automatic farms. That means the farm can run on its own.

Players have also made elevators and computers. They even made a guitar.

Minecraft grows and changes. With each change, players will be able to come up with new creations that use redstone.

Minecraft players can try many things in the game.

Real-Life Redstone

Redstone circuits need an input and an output to work. An input, such as a button or lever, allows power to go into the circuit. The output is the item receiving the power, such as a door or torch. People use computer programs at work and school. Like redstone circuits, computer programs use inputs and outputs. People input data with a keyboard or mouse. Outputs can be items such as text or sound.

Glossary

circuit: the path an electric current flows through

Creative Mode: a freestyle block-building mode in *Minecraft*

material: anything used for building something

mob: animals and monsters in *Minecraft*

piston: a block that can push other blocks when moved by redstone

sensor: a device that responds to a change in the environment, such as light

virtual: existing on a computer

Learn More

Gregory, Josh. *Redstone and Transportation in Minecraft*. Ann Arbor, MI: Cherry Lake, 2019.

Introduction to Redstone
http://www.minecraft101.net/redstone/redstone-basics.html

Keppeler, Sam. *The Unofficial Guide to Using Tools in* Minecraft. New York: PowerKids, 2020.

Leed, Percy. Minecraft *Construction: An Unofficial Kids' Guide*. Minneapolis: Lerner Publications, 2023.

Minecraft Official Site
https://www.minecraft.net/en-us

Minecraft Wiki: Redstone
https://minecraft-archive.fandom.com/wiki/Redstone

Index

Photo Acknowledgments

Image credits: Various screenshots by Heather Schwartz, Linda Zajac, and Julia Zajac; Leonidas Santana/Shutterstock, p. 4; Bloomicon/Shutterstock, p. 20.

Cover: Linda Zajac.